ARIZONA

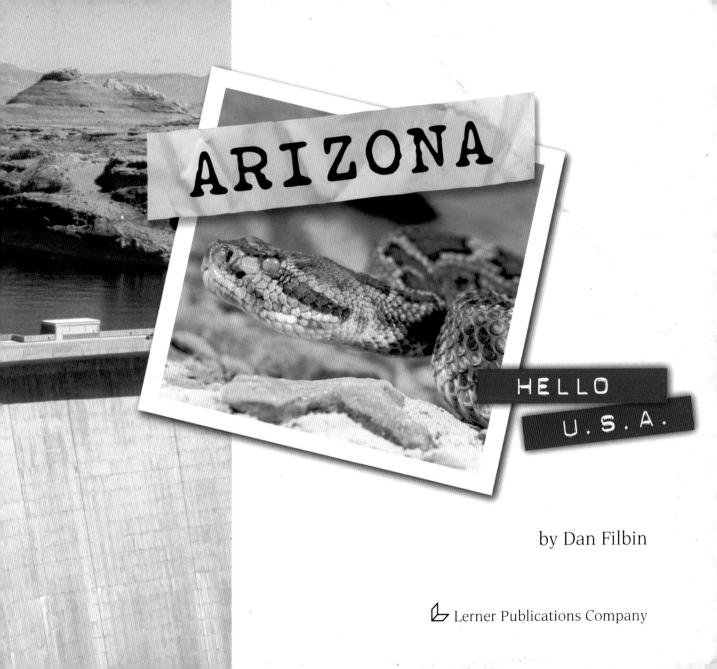

ARIZONA

HELLO
U.S.A.

by Dan Filbin

Lerner Publications Company

You'll find this picture of a Navajo rug at the beginning of every chapter. Many Navajo Indians in Arizona make these colorful rugs from start to finish—they raise sheep for wool, grow plants to make dyes, spin the wool into thread, and then weave the rugs. The patterns on the rugs can symbolize seasons, animals, landforms, or aspects of Navajo life, but sometimes they're simply attractive designs.

Cover (left): Phoenix at sunset. Cover (right): Saguaro cactus near Baboquivari Peak in south central Arizona. Pages 2–3: Glen Canyon Dam, on the Colorado River in north central Arizona. Page 3: Arizona black rattlesnake.

This book is available in two editions:
Library binding by Lerner Publications Company, a division of Lerner Publishing Group
Soft cover by First Avenue Editions, an imprint of Lerner Publishing Group
241 First Avenue North
Minneapolis, MN 55401 U.S.A.

Website address: www.lernerbooks.com

Library of Congress Cataloging-in-Publication Data

Filbin, Dan, 1951–
    Arizona / by Dan Filbin. (Rev. and expanded 2nd ed.)
      p.   cm. — (Hello U.S.A.)
    Includes index.
    Summary: Introduces the geography, history, economy, famous people, and environment of the Grand Canyon State.
    ISBN: 0–8225–4063–0 (lib. bdg. : alk paper)
    ISBN: 0–8225–4133–5 (pbk. : alk. paper)
    1. Arizona—Juvenile literature. [1. Arizona.] I. Title. II. Series.
    F811.3 .F55 2002
    979.1—dc21   2001002961

Manufactured in the United States of America
1 2 3 4 5 6 – JR – 07 06 05 04 03 02

CONTENTS

Many kinds of cactus grow in Organ Pipe Cactus National Monument near Ajo, Arizona. Saguaro cacti have arms, and organ pipe cacti grow straight with no arms.

THE LAND

Canyons and Cacti

eserts, forests, and mountains make Arizona a place full of wonders. Its most famous treasure—the Grand Canyon— gives the state its nickname, the Grand Canyon State. Much of this land in the southwestern United States looks as if it has been splashed with rich red, brown, and green paints.

At its northeastern corner, Arizona touches New Mexico, Colorado, and Utah. Mexico borders Arizona on the south, and California and Nevada lie to the west. The state has three geographic regions—the Northern Plateau, the Central Mountains, and the Southern Desert.

The early morning sun casts a reddish glow on this sandstone bluff.

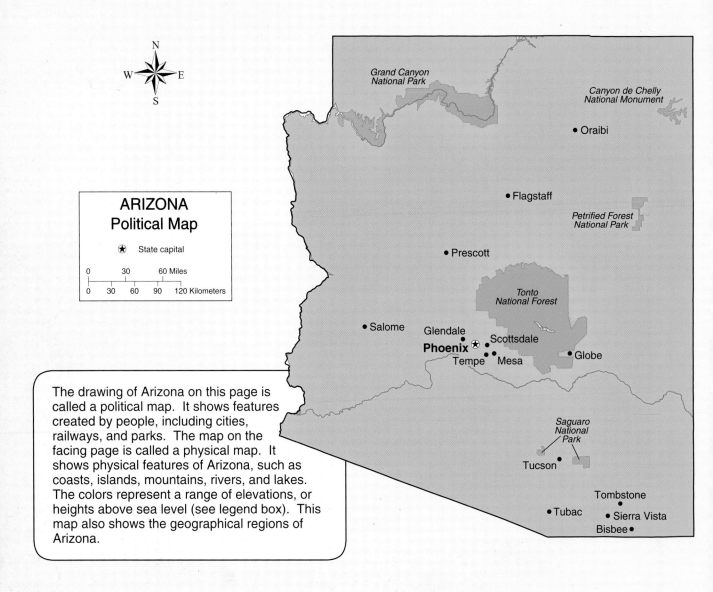

ARIZONA
Political Map

⊛ State capital

0   30   60 Miles
0   30   60   90   120 Kilometers

Grand Canyon
National Park

Canyon de Chelly
National Monument

• Oraibi

• Flagstaff

Petrified Forest
National Park

• Prescott

Tonto
National Forest

• Salome

Glendale
•
Phoenix ⊛   • Scottsdale
           •   •
       Tempe • Mesa   • Globe

Saguaro
National
Park

• Tucson

Tombstone
•

• Tubac   • Sierra Vista
Bisbee •

The drawing of Arizona on this page is called a political map. It shows features created by people, including cities, railways, and parks. The map on the facing page is called a physical map. It shows physical features of Arizona, such as coasts, islands, mountains, rivers, and lakes. The colors represent a range of elevations, or heights above sea level (see legend box). This map also shows the geographical regions of Arizona.

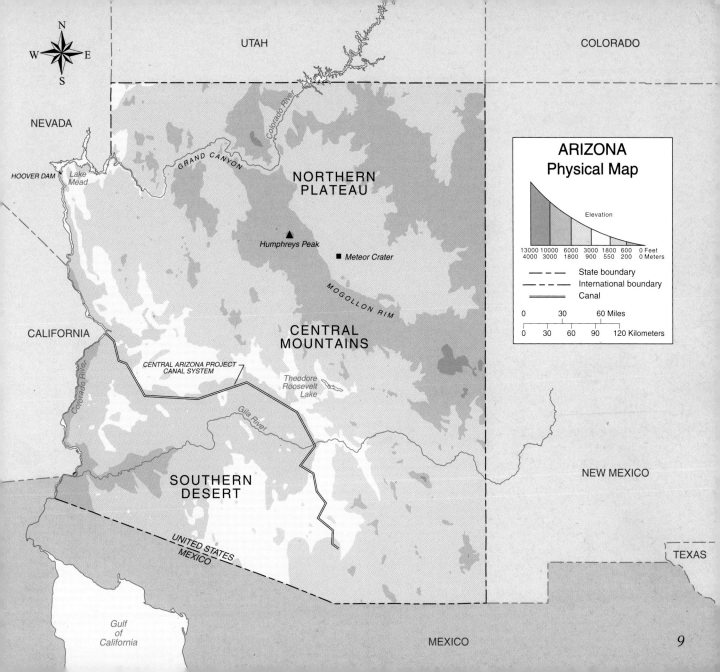

N
W E
S

UTAH

COLORADO

NEVADA

Colorado River

GRAND CANYON

HOOVER DAM

Lake
Mead

NORTHERN
PLATEAU

▲ Humphreys Peak

■ *Meteor Crater*

MOGOLLON RIM

CALIFORNIA

CENTRAL
MOUNTAINS

Colorado River

CENTRAL ARIZONA PROJECT
CANAL SYSTEM

*Theodore
Roosevelt
Lake*

Gila River

SOUTHERN
DESERT

NEW MEXICO

UNITED STATES
MEXICO

TEXAS

*Gulf
of
California*

MEXICO

ARIZONA
Physical Map

Elevation

| 13000 | 10000 | 6000 | 3000 | 1800 | 600 | 0 Feet |
| 4000 | 3000 | 1800 | 900 | 550 | 200 | 0 Meters |

— · — State boundary

— — — International boundary

═══ Canal

0   30   60 Miles

0   30   60   90   120 Kilometers

Wind has sculpted sand and rock into many amazing shapes on Arizona's Northern Plateau.

The Northern Plateau, which is actually a series of **plateaus** (flat highlands), makes up two-fifths of Arizona. Over time, winds on the Northern Plateau have sculpted the reddish-brown rock into shapes that look like towering needles and huge tabletops. Humphreys Peak, on the southern edge of the plateau region, reaches 12,633 feet and is the state's highest point.

Rivers have cut **canyons** (steep valleys) into the Northern Plateau. The Colorado River began carving the longest and deepest of Arizona's canyons, the Grand Canyon, more than a million years ago. The valley is about 1 mile deep in some places.

Strong winds and water from the Colorado River have worn down the land over millions of years, creating the Grand Canyon.

The mountains of southern Arizona offer many trails for horseback riders to enjoy.

As the Colorado River cuts still deeper into the valley, the newly exposed layers of rock reveal more and more of the earth's history.

The Mogollon Rim—a rock cliff 200 miles long—divides the Northern Plateau from the Central Mountains. Millions of years ago, volcanoes and earthquakes formed these mountain peaks.

Forests cast a green hue on the Central Mountains. You may imagine only **deserts** when you think of Arizona, but trees cover one-fifth of the state. In fact, Arizona has the largest stands of ponderosa pine in the United States. In the Southern Desert,

Ponderosa pines grow well in the mountainous areas of central Arizona.

gently sloping valleys made of rock and sand separate the region's mountain ranges. The desert is dry most of the year. But during the rainy period from July through September, many valleys turn briefly into shallow basins of water. The Southern Desert gets most of its yearly moisture during these three months.

Even though the desert gets little rain, some plants grow well there. Mesquite, ironwood, and paloverde trees thrive on the craggy slopes. The long-armed saguaro and the spiny cholla are among the wide variety of cacti found in the Southern Desert.

The dry streambeds in Arizona's Central Mountains fill with rushing water when the snow melts.

Two major rivers flow through Arizona. The Colorado River travels through the northwestern part of the state before cutting south to form most of Arizona's western boundary. The Gila River crosses the southern width of the state and then joins the Colorado River in the southwest.

Arizona has a warm and sunny climate. In many parts of the state, the sun shines about 8 out of 10 days. Temperatures vary widely in the state because of differences in elevation. On summer days in the Southern Desert, the hottest region, the thermometer often tops 100° F. But in the Central Mountains, the highest region, temperatures range from 70° to 80° F.

In the summer, thunderstorm clouds often bring sudden, hard downpours. Less threatening winter rains occur from December through March throughout much of Arizona. After rains fall, the tangy odor of the creosote bush fills the air in many parts of the state.

The saguaro cactus, native to Arizona's Southern Desert, can grow to a height of 60 feet. The plant is the largest cactus in the United States.

In July and August, short and intense downpours sometimes drench Arizona.

Prickly pear cactus *(left)* and barrel cactus *(right)* grow in Arizona's deserts.

The Southern Desert's Gila monsters—lizards that are 18 inches long—are the only poisonous lizards in the United States. But they are not as dangerous as 1-inch-long scorpions from the same region.

So many people live in certain areas of Arizona that some animals that once roamed the state have died out. But white-tailed deer and pronghorn antelope still range through the less populated areas.

Indians created these drawings of people, animals, and plants on rocks in northeastern Arizona more than a thousand years ago.

THE HISTORY

Maize, Missions, and Mines

The first people to live in North America came from Asia about 40,000 years ago. Traveling in groups, they crossed over the land that then connected Asia and North America in the northern Pacific Ocean. The descendants of these people are known as Indians, or Native Americans.

For thousands of years, these groups from Asia spread throughout North and South America. Some of the tribes began moving into the region that later became Arizona about 12,000 years ago. At first they hunted herds of large animals for food. Tracking the herds kept them on the move for many months of the year.

Indian farmers stored maize, a type of corn that is easily preserved.

Around 2000 B.C., the Indians learned to grow grains and vegetables from tribes in the area that later became Mexico. Maize, known as corn in the United States, became a main part of their diet. These farming Indians lived together in permanent settlements and relied on hunting less and less. **Archaeologists** have discovered beautifully crafted tools, baskets, and pottery at sites where hunting camps and farming villages once stood. Some of the objects were carved and painted with pictures of animals and human figures that represented spirits.

This irrigation canal was built by Hohokam Indians about 1,500 years ago.

In the A.D. 500s, an Indian people called the Hohokam built canals to carry water from the Gila River. A form of **irrigation,** this process provided enough water to make maize and other crops grow more easily in the dry climate. The Hohokam constructed about 250 miles of canals, some of which measured 15 feet deep and 30 feet wide. Several of these canals are still used by farmers.

By A.D. 800, another tribe, known as the Anasazi, had constructed homes that resemble modern apartment buildings. Using stone and mud, these people made square dwellings that were attached to each other. Sometimes the buildings were several stories high, and some were built into the sides of towering cliffs. As many as 1,000 people lived together in some Anasazi communities.

The Anasazi began construction of this village around A.D. 1250. In modern times, it is known as the Betatakin Ruin and contains about 135 rooms.

The White House Ruin lies along a stream in Canyon de Chelly. Ten rooms are built into the face of the huge rock cliff, and about 60 rooms are located near the stream. These buildings probably housed 100 people and were constructed in about A.D. 1060 by the Anasazi.

Long periods without rain occurred in the late 1200s. The three main groups of Indians in Arizona (the Mogollon, the Hohokam, and the Anasazi) left their large settlements and formed smaller communities. Living in groups of fewer people made it easier for the Indians to grow enough food to feed themselves.

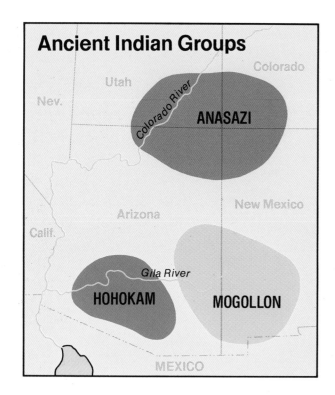

Ancient Indian Groups

The Anasazi, Hohokam, and Mogollon eventually traded goods with each other and shared farming methods. This map shows where these ancient Indian groups lived in A.D. 1000.

The Apache and the Navajo moved into what later became Arizona probably during the 1200s or 1300s. They came originally from the northwestern part of North America. These Indians specialized in hunting animals. To get food and other supplies, they also carried out raids on people who lived nearby.

In the 1500s, Spaniards in search of gold explored the region that later became Arizona. Marcos de Niza, a Catholic priest, traveled through the region in 1539, and Francisco Vásquez de Coronado led another expedition the next year. Neither Coronado

nor Niza found golden cities. Members of Coronado's group, however, were the first Europeans to discover the Grand Canyon.

Spanish settlers soon followed the earliest Spanish explorers to the region. By 1598 Spaniards had moved to the area, which included Mexico as well as Arizona. Spanish leaders set up a government, making a **colony** called New Spain. Colonial leaders received their instructions from faraway Spain.

This drawing shows a Hopi religious ceremony. The Hopi Indians are related to the Anasazi group.

Eusebio Kino and his followers began to build the church of San Xavier del Bac in 1700. They used clay bricks that had been dried in the sun. The church was rebuilt in 1783 with fire-hardened brick.

Visitors enter the church of
San Xavier del Bac near Tucson.

In the 1690s, the Spanish sent
another Catholic priest, Eusebio Kino,
to build a church. This church was
known as San Xavier del Bac. At the
villages he visited in the area, Kino
worked as a **missionary,** introducing
Indians to the Christian religion. He
also taught them new ways of raising
livestock, fruit trees, and grain. Kino
had learned some of these methods from Indians in
southern New Spain.

Not all Indians accepted the missionaries or the
Spanish soldiers who came with them. The
Spaniards used the Indians as manual laborers to
build churches and forts and to grow food. Many
Indians did not want to give up their original
religion, and they fought to keep the lands that
the Spaniards wanted to take from them.

Like their Hohokam ancestors, the Pima Indians became skillful farmers.

At first, Apache and Navajo raiders moved about the territory on foot. But as they captured horses from the Spanish troops, these Indians became even better fighters because they were able to attack and retreat quickly. For protection, the Spanish built forts of **adobe** (bricks of dried clay) at Tubac, Tucson, and other places.

Indian attacks at the end of the 1700s and the beginning of the 1800s drove many Spaniards from settlements in northern New Spain. The Spanish colonial government had less control than before, and Indian leaders saw an opportunity to overthrow Spanish rule. These rebels won independence in 1821, and the lands of Arizona became part of the new nation of Mexico.

Adobe villages, like this one at Navajo National Monument, were used as homes and as protection.

In the next 25 years, many U.S. citizens settled in the northern Mexican territory—which included land in what later became Arizona, New Mexico, and California. Border disputes between the United States and Mexico led to war over the boundary between the two countries.

After the Mexican-American War, a **treaty** (peace agreement) signed in 1848 required Mexico to give up some of its territory. According to the agreement, northern Arizona became part of the United States. Then in 1853 the United States bought land from Mexico through the Gadsden Purchase. This new piece of U.S. property included the southern part of Arizona.

This territory was far enough south for an east-west postal route to stay open even in winter. Stagecoach drivers and riders on horseback carried the mail across Arizona. Harsh weather made the route difficult for these early postal carriers. Attacks by white outlaws and small groups of Indian raiders were also a constant threat. Mail stations were built along the way to give the postal carriers added protection.

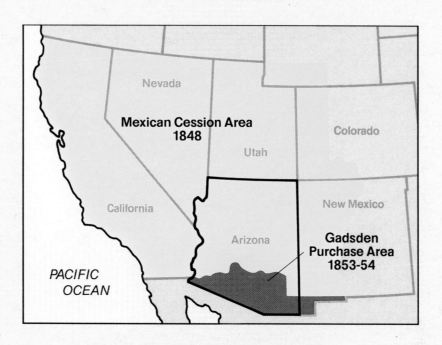

Map showing:
- Nevada
- Mexican Cession Area 1848
- Utah
- Colorado
- California
- New Mexico
- Arizona
- Gadsden Purchase Area 1853-54
- PACIFIC OCEAN

Arizona's Growth

The United States acquired the area that later became Arizona from Mexico during the mid-1800s. After the Mexican-American War, Mexico gave the United States some of its land, including parts of what later became Arizona, Colorado, New Mexico, California, Wyoming, and Nevada. Then, in 1853, the United States made the Gadsden Purchase. James Gadsden, the U.S. minister to Mexico, arranged for the United States to buy the land south of the Gila River from Mexico for $10 million. By 1854 all of the area that later became Arizona was owned by the United States. It was actually part of New Mexico Territory at the time— Arizona did not become its own territory until 1863.

Until 1864, the rambling Canyon de Chelly provided a place of safety for Navajo who opposed the U.S. government.

Fighting known as the Indian Wars broke out between Indians and U.S. troops from 1860 to 1886. Some Indians went on raids to get food and supplies, but they also fought to keep control of their homelands as more U.S. troops arrived. Kit Carson, an officer in the army, led U.S. soldiers against the Navajo. The army defeated these Indians at Canyon de Chelly in 1864.

Goyathlay *(front row, third from right)* and members of his Apache tribe are permitted a rest stop while traveling by train to a reservation.

Apache fighters continued to raid the residents of Arizona for several years after the Navajo were defeated. Goyathlay (also known as Geronimo), Cochise, and Mangas Coloradas—Apache leaders— launched swift and daring attacks on other Indian tribes as well as on white settlers. By retreating into the rough deserts and mountains, the Apache often avoided capture. But they were greatly outnumbered by U.S. troops.

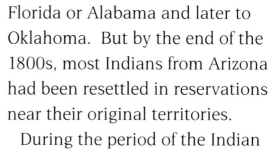

Goyathlay and his followers surrendered in 1886. Most of the captured Apache warriors and their families were sent to **reservations.** When the Indians arrived at these territories that had been set aside for them, they found that some of the areas were quite unlike their homelands.

A small number of the Apache were sent to Florida or Alabama and later to Oklahoma. But by the end of the 1800s, most Indians from Arizona had been resettled in reservations near their original territories.

During the period of the Indian Wars, a few prospectors found large amounts of silver and copper in Arizona. These discoveries drew many more people to the region.

New towns grew quickly and were often crowded with residents who

Arizona's prospectors searched for precious minerals in the desert ground.

had recently made fortunes. Several settlements in Arizona—for example, Tombstone and Bisbee—gained reputations as tough western towns, where disagreements were sometimes settled by brawls and gunfights.

The number of farmers and ranchers also multiplied during this time. Cowboys tended herds of livestock on Arizona's wide, open land. When the cattle were ready to be sold, cowboys took the animals by means of cattle drives to markets in California or the Midwest. These drives sometimes had herds of 4,000 or more.

Arizona's open landscape made it an excellent place for cattle ranching in the late 1800s.

35

By the 1870s, ranchers, prospectors, and others had settled large parts of Arizona, and they began to think about statehood. But it was not until 1912 that the U.S. government accepted Arizona's constitution. The new state was the 48th to join the Union.

The state's first governor, George W. P. Hunt, worked hard to help Arizona's farms and businesses grow. Hunt set aside some of the state's money to build roads and dams. The dams blocked the flow of rivers to collect water for irrigation. Watering their fields through irrigation allowed farmers to till more land. Crops such as cotton became a major part of the state's economy.

During World War II (1939–1945), Arizona's population grew quickly. The state's warm weather and clear flying conditions made it a good place to test airplanes and to train pilots. Airplane manufacturers and military bases moved into the region, drawing many new workers to the state. As the farms and copper mines expanded, more people came to Arizona to pick cotton or dig for valuable minerals.

Arizona was admitted to the Union in 1912. In that year, the first group of state lawmakers met in Phoenix.

Arizona is home to several military bases. These jets wait for action at a holding facility in Flagstaff.

Arizona's population continued to grow rapidly after World War II. In the 40 years from 1940 to 1980, the number of Arizonans increased by more than four times. People came from other parts of the United States and from Mexico to work on the farms, in the mines, or in new factories. Many retired people also moved to the state. Arizona remains one of the fastest growing states in the country. In fact, between 1990 and 2000, its population increased by 40 percent. Only Nevada's population grew at a faster pace during that time.

During the late 1980s and 1990s, Arizona experienced some political troubles. Governor Evan Mecham was impeached, or removed from office, in 1988 for illegal use of the state's money. And in 1997, Governor Fife Symington resigned from office because of crimes he committed before becoming governor. Despite these problems, Arizonans, both longtime residents and newcomers, try to make their state a welcoming place.

Many people retire to Arizona due to its warm climate and friendly communities.

Arizona's second largest city—Tucson—has a population of more than 480,000 people and is still growing.

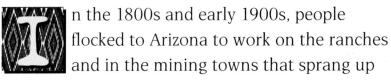

PEOPLE & ECONOMY

Ranches and Rodeos

A dancer celebrates his Indian heritage.

In the 1800s and early 1900s, people flocked to Arizona to work on the ranches and in the mining towns that sprang up almost overnight. People no longer come to the state in large numbers to work on the land or in the mines, but Arizona's population is still growing fast. One out of four residents has moved to the state since 1990. By 2000, about 5.1 million people were living in Arizona.

About 25 percent of Arizonans are people of Latin American ancestry. Three percent of the state's residents are black, and 64 percent are white. Almost 5 percent of Arizonans are Native American. A small percentage of Arizonan people are of Asian ancestry.

Phoenix's Heard Museum displays statues of Navajo people in traditional clothing.

Most Arizonans live and work in cities and towns, and about half live in Phoenix, the capital city, and its neighboring communities. Tucson, farther to the south, is Arizona's second largest city.

Phoenix and Tucson are the state's largest cultural centers. Among the museums in these two cities are some that display the history of the West. Other attractions include the Champlin Fighter Museum, which exhibits combat planes from the two world wars.

Still other museums have collections of artwork gathered from many parts of the world. The most popular exhibits, however, feature the art of Arizonans, especially that of potters influenced by ancient Indian traditions. Several nature museums,

Dancers perform in colorful Mexican dress during a fiesta.

such as the Arizona-Sonora Desert Museum near Tucson, show how the region's plants and animals live in the desert climate.

People in dozens of towns throughout Arizona celebrate their past by holding festivals, rodeos, or fairs. Flagstaff hosts the All-Indian Pow Wow, and the mining town of Globe puts on the Copper Dust Stampede Rodeo. Tucson recalls yesterday's cowboys and cowgirls and tests the skill of modern ranch hands during the Fiesta de los Vaqueros.

Indian Reservations in Arizona

So many immigrants have swelled Arizona's population that the state's original residents—Native Americans—make up only about 5 percent of the population. More than 233,000 Indians live in Arizona, giving the state the third largest population of Native Americans in the country. About three out of four of Arizona's Native Americans live on one of the state's 22 reservations. More than one-fourth of Arizona's land is covered by Indian reservations.

The largest Indian territory, the Navajo Indian Reservation, covers more than 13 million acres in north-eastern Arizona. About 170,000 Navajo live on this reservation. A neighboring tribe—the Hopi—have their own reservation and share the use of some of the Navajo land. Other large reservations in Arizona include Fort Apache and Gila River, each with a population of about 10,000 people.

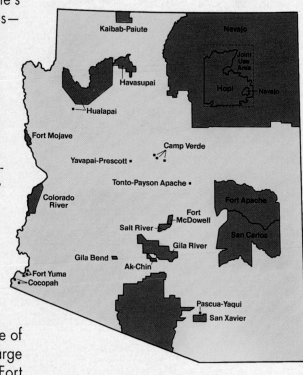

Kaibab-Paiute

Navajo

Joint Use Area

Havasupai

Hopi — Navajo

Hualapai

Fort Mojave

Camp Verde

Yavapai-Prescott

Tonto-Payson Apache

Colorado River

Fort Apache

Fort McDowell

Salt River

San Carlos

Gila River

Gila Bend

Ak-Chin

Fort Yuma
Cocopah

Pascua-Yaqui

San Xavier

This painting, created by a Hopi artist, shows dancers performing the Hopi corn dance. This ceremony is held during the summer months to help crops grow better and to bring people closer together.

Many Arizonans enjoy attending sports events. The Phoenix Coyotes began playing in the National Hockey League (NHL) in 1996. The Arizona Cardinals of the National Football League (NFL) currently play their home games at Arizona State University's stadium. (A new stadium in Tempe is scheduled to open in 2004.) Arizona also has a National Basketball Association (NBA) team, the Phoenix Suns, and a Major League Baseball (MLB) team called the Arizona Diamondbacks. Several major league baseball teams also hold spring training in the state.

Basketball fans enjoy watching the Phoenix Suns compete.

Other favorite activities of Arizonans include camping and boating. Lake Mead in the western part of the state and Theodore Roosevelt Lake northeast of Phoenix are two popular spots for fishing. These and other artificial lakes were created when Arizonans built dams on some of their rivers to collect water for irrigation.

Over two-thirds of the people who work in Arizona earn their livelihoods by providing services. People with service jobs work in restaurants, stores, and banks. Another large group of workers holds jobs in factories. Airplane parts, concrete blocks, parts for computers, and printed materials are some of the items that the state's industries produce.

Mining provides still other jobs in the state. Miners dig for copper and silver in southern Arizona. Earnings from these minerals were large for many years, but since the 1980s they have provided less of the state's income. By the late 1990s, mining was earning only 1 percent of the money in the state. Uranium (a fuel used in nuclear energy) and coal are mined mostly in the north. Some regions of the state have plenty of sand and gravel, which are used to make roads and buildings.

Arizona's warm climate attracts millions of tourists, including a large number of retired people. Tourists golf on the state's many courses *(above)* and spend time at resorts *(left)*.

The desert landscape of Arizona provides a backdrop for many movies set in the Wild West *(above)*. The state is also a center for development of new airplane technology *(right)*.

Irrigation and a long growing season help Arizona's crops thrive. Most farms are in the southern part of the state. The main crops include cotton, wheat, citrus fruits, pecans, and dates. Arizona's farms produce more cotton per acre than those in any other state. This is partly because they can grow more than one crop in a year.

Unlike people in many other states, who use plows to shovel snow, Arizonans use them to gather sand for use in construction.

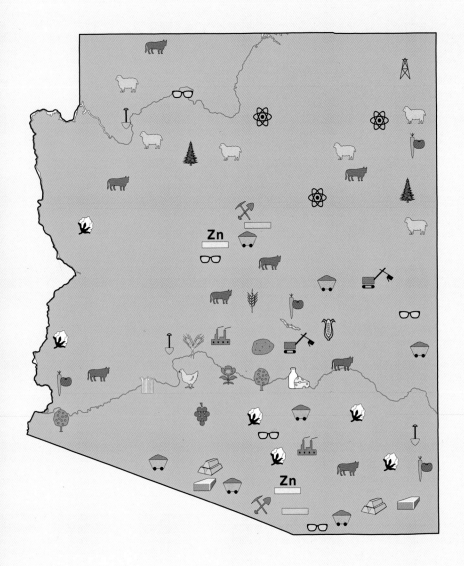

ARIZONA
Economic Map

The symbols on this map show where different economic activities take place in Arizona. The legend below explains what each symbol stands for.

	Barley		Manufacturing
	Beef cattle		Nursery products
	Corn		Oil
	Copper		Potatoes
	Cotton		Poultry
	Dairy products		Sand and gravel
	Forest products		Sheep
	Fruit		Silver
	Gold		Stone
	Grapes		Tourism
	Hay		Uranium
	Iron ore		Vegetables
	Lead		Wheat

Zn Zinc

The number of jobs in Arizona grew quickly during the early 1980s. By the end of the decade, however, a large number of residents—both new and longtime— were having a hard time finding work. During the mid- and late 1990s, however, Arizona's economy became stronger. Many people continue to come to Arizona, and state leaders are working to continue developing more opportunities for employment.

The Northern Plateau is the center of agriculture in Arizona. This rancher herds goats to another feeding area.

Courthouse Rock points majestically toward the sky in Eagletail Mountains Wilderness Area, west of Phoenix. Like most of Arizona, the area is very dry, and plants and people there must conserve water to survive.

THE ENVIRONMENT

Stretching the Water Supply

Water is Arizona's most precious resource. At one time, the state had enough water to supply its people, plants, and animals easily. As the number of Arizonans increases, the demand for water also grows. Simple activities such as watering the lawn or taking a shower, when done by more and more people, can quickly use up much of the state's valuable supply of water.

Some of the ways people use Arizona's water have caused several plants and animals to become extinct, or die out. Others are in danger of becoming extinct. For example, about 70 percent of Arizona's native species of fish are threatened because dams or other building projects are destroying or altering the streams in which the fish live.

Located on the Colorado River, the Hoover Dam holds back enough water to form Lake Mead. At its base, the dam is two football fields thick (660 feet).

Even without the environmental changes caused by humans, the plants and animals of Arizona already face the difficulties of a hot, dry environment. To help them survive, these plants and animals have very effective ways of using and storing water.

Mesquite trees, for example, grow deep roots to

Pumping too much water from underground can cause the soil to collapse, leaving cracks in the earth.

tap sources of water far underground. Many cacti have long roots, too, but they often spread out near the surface of the desert soil. When it rains, the root system is in position to drink in as much moisture as possible. This ability is crucial, since water is necessary for life.

People also need water. But some of the ways people collect and use water harm the environment. Arizonans have pumped out large amounts of **groundwater** (water from underground) to get more water for agriculture and for use in cities. Almost 85 percent of this water is used to grow crops.

So much groundwater has been removed that some land is starting to sink. Even if people completely stopped using groundwater, this resource would take thousands of years to refill itself.

Arizonans have recognized for several decades that water is in short supply. In the 1940s, state leaders began planning the Central Arizona Project, a system of dams, pumps, and canals that takes water from the Colorado River to Phoenix and Tucson. Construction on the project began in the 1970s and was completed in 1991.

Part of the Central Arizona Project, this canal carries water across the Southern Desert from the Colorado River.

The Colorado River, which provides a natural habitat for many animals and fish, is losing water faster than it can be replaced.

This project brings needed water to homes, businesses, and farms in south central Arizona, but it also has drawbacks. Lakes created by the dams have covered large pieces of land, destroying the original plant life and the homes of many animals. Canals make artificial barriers that prevent some wildlife from roaming their usual territories and feeding.

Not all of Arizona's people benefit from the project. In 1995, because of problems with the pipes in an older section of Tucson, Tucson voters passed a law that limited the use of Central Arizona Project water until 2000, unless the water met quality standards. The water wasn't clean enough, and Tucson went back to using groundwater. This caused the city's groundwater to run dangerously short. In 2001 the city began to mix a small amount of water from the Central Arizona Project with its groundwater.

Arizonans are working to protect the unique natural beauty of their state.

The Central Arizona Project may damage the Colorado River and its wildlife. Millions of gallons of water are removed from the Colorado River each day. This lowers the river's total water—a practice that leaves the land downstream without the water it needs. Moving water from one place to another means that some people will get less water so that others can have more. Plants and animals are also greatly affected by this environmental change.

With many communities expanding and new ones springing up, Arizona's growth has a big impact on the environment. Arizonans are trying to protect their environment and, at the same time, keep the state growing.

To do this, people are thinking of ways to stretch their water supply. For example, farmers are looking

for ways to raise crops with less water, and city planners are trying to figure out more ways to recycle water that has already been used in factories and homes. The state's deserts, mountains, and plateaus—and the water that supports the life in them—must be cared for wisely.

Caring for Arizona's water supply will help the state's wildlife—and its economy—to thrive.

ALL ABOUT ARIZONA

Fun Facts

Some of the rock in the deepest parts of Arizona's Grand Canyon is almost 2 billion years old.

People have lived at Oraibi, Arizona, longer than at any other site in the United States. Hopi Indians and their Anasazi ancestors have lived at Oraibi for more than 800 years.

About 50,000 years ago, a giant meteorite (a chunk of stone from space) struck the earth near the area that later became Flagstaff, Arizona. The hole the meteorite gouged, known as Meteor Crater, is 570 feet deep and nearly a mile wide.

The name Arizona comes from an ancient Native American word, *arizonac*, that probably means "small springs."

Wild camels once roamed Arizona's deserts. During the 1850s, the U.S. Army brought the animals from the Middle East to the southwestern United States, thinking that camels could easily carry goods across the desert. The experiment failed—the camels didn't adapt well to the area's rocky desert ground. Some of them escaped in Arizona, where they wandered free for years. The last wild Arizona camel was captured and sent to a zoo in 1905.

Arizona is one of the only states to have official neckwear. The bola tie was created by Vic Cedarstaff, a silversmith, in 1949. It became Arizona's official neckwear in 1971.

These children are exploring one of Arizona's springs.

STATE SONG

Arizona's state song was written in 1915 and adopted in 1919.

ARIZONA MARCH SONG

Music by Maurice Blumenthal; words by Margaret Rowe Clifford

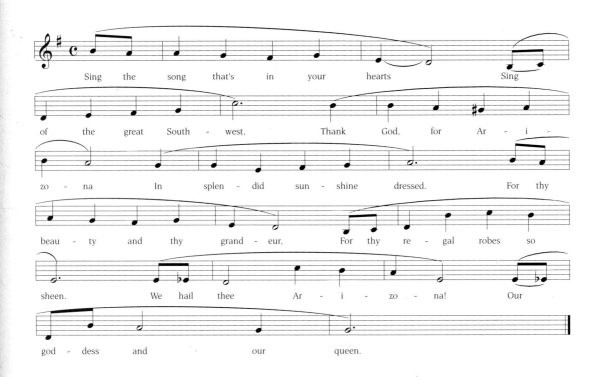

You can hear "Arizona March Song" by visiting this website:
<http://www.50states.com/songs/arizona.htm>

AN ARIZONA RECIPE

Citrus trees are grown throughout Arizona, bearing grapefruits, oranges, lemons, and other fruits. This simple salad recipe uses several Arizona fruits.

GRAPEFRUIT SALAD

2 large grapefruit
peel of 1 orange, cut in thin strips
1 red onion, thinly sliced
juice of 1 lemon
1 garlic clove, finely chopped
½ teaspoon salt

1 teaspoon mustard (preferably Dijon)
½ cup olive oil
¼ cup orange juice
pepper (preferably freshly ground)
½ cup watercress leaves

1. Peel the grapefruit, divide into segments, and remove the rind from each piece.
2. Place segments in a serving bowl. (Should be approximately 3 cups of grapefruit.)
3. Place onions and orange peels on top of grapefruit.
4. In a separate bowl, mash the garlic and the salt together.
5. Slowly stirring, add olive oil, mustard, and orange and lemon juice to the garlic and salt mixture.
6. Pour entire mixture over grapefruit.
7. Add pepper to taste.
8. Chill completely and top with watercress leaves.

HISTORICAL TIMELINE

10,000 B.C. Indians begin arriving in the region later known as Arizona.

A.D. 500s The Hohokam Indians build canals in southern Arizona.

800 The Anasazi construct homes that resemble the shape of modern apartment buildings.

1200–1400 Apache and Navajo Indians enter the region.

1539 Marcos de Niza is the first European to travel in Arizona.

1598 Spanish leaders set up a colony called New Spain, which includes the area that later became Arizona.

1692 Eusebio Francisco Kino founds the church of San Xavier del Bac; construction begins in 1700.

1821 The lands of Arizona become part of Mexico.

1848 Northern Arizona is added to the United States after the Mexican War (1846–1848).

1853 The United States buys southern Arizona in the Gadsden Purchase.

1860 The Indian Wars begin and continue until 1886.

1864 The U.S. Army defeats the Navajo at Canyon de Chelly.

1870 Ranchers and prospectors settle in Arizona.

1886 Goyathlay (Geronimo) and his people surrender to U.S. troops.

1912 Arizona becomes the 48th state.

1936 The Hoover Dam, Arizona's first major dam, is completed.

1939 Arizona's population grows quickly with the start of World War II.

1984 Arizona has the second-fastest population growth in the United States.

1988 Governor Evan Mecham is impeached.

1997 Governor Fife Symington resigns.

2001 U.S. census data show that, after 60 years of rapid growth, Arizona's population has reached 5,130,000.

OUTSTANDING ARIZONANS

Byrd Baylor

Erma Bombeck

Raul Castro

William Croft Barnes (1853–1936) was awarded the Congressional Medal of Honor in 1881 for his courage as a scout during battles against the Apache.

Byrd Baylor (born 1924) grew up on ranches and in mining towns in Texas and Arizona. A resident of Tucson, she writes books for children that explore the natural beauty of the Southwest. Some of her books tell about the life and culture of the region's Native Americans. Baylor has won several honors for her work, including prizes for *The Desert Is Theirs* and *The Way to Start a Day.*

Erma Bombeck (1927–1996) wrote a funny newspaper column about the trials of family life. She also wrote several best-selling books, including *I Want to Grow Hair, I Want to Grow Up, I Want to Go to Boise*—a book about children who have survived cancer. She and her family moved to Arizona in 1971.

Lynda Carter (born 1951) grew up in Phoenix and became an actress and singer. She starred in the television series *Wonder Woman* during the late 1970s.

Raul H. Castro (born 1916) became the first Mexican-American governor of Arizona. He was elected in 1974. Castro also has served as a U.S. official in several Central and South American countries.

Cesar Chavez (1927–1993) grew up in Yuma, Arizona. In 1962 he organized a labor union for farmers called the National Farm Workers Association. Chavez helped improve living conditions and raise wages for migrant farmworkers throughout the southwestern United States.

Cesar Chavez

Cochise (1812?–1874) was an Apache chief who led his warriors in successful battles against settlers and U.S. troops in Arizona. For more than 10 years, he and his followers used their knowledge of the mountains to avoid the soldiers who were pursuing them.

Cochise

George Crook (1829–1890) led the U.S. Army in Arizona during its conflicts with the Apache in the 1870s and 1880s. Crook tried to convince the government to settle Arizona's Indians on reservations near their home territory.

George Crook

Andrew E. Douglas (1867–1962) worked for many years as an astronomer and public official. He also studied prehistoric life in Arizona and discovered a way to date ruins by measuring the age of the wood that is found at ancient sites.

John Charles Frémont (1813–1890) explored large parts of the western United States, including Arizona. He was also a Union general during the Civil War and governor of the Territory of Arizona from 1878 to 1881.

John Charles Frémont

Barry M. Goldwater (1909–1998) was a native of Phoenix, where his family owned a business for many years. He served on the city council and later became a U.S. senator. He was elected as a senator five times, serving a total of 30 years. In the 1964 presidential election, Goldwater ran as the candidate of the Republican Party but lost to his Democratic opponent, Lyndon B. Johnson.

Barry Goldwater

Goyathlay

Zane Grey

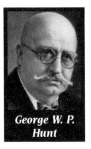
George W. P. Hunt

Eusebio Kino

Goyathlay (1829–1909), renamed Geronimo by Spanish settlers, was an Apache leader and skillful warrior. He led swift attacks on settlers and soldiers and retreated quickly into Arizona's deserts and rugged mountains. He and his band surrendered to U.S. Army troops in 1886.

John C. Greenway (1872–1926) fought in both the Spanish-American War and World War I. He was one of the first people to successfully develop Arizona's copper mines in the early 1900s.

Zane Grey (1875–1939) wrote novels about the Wild West. He visited Arizona often and lived for a time in Oak Creek Canyon, drawing many of the details of his books from Arizona's landscape. Some of his titles are *Riders of the Purple Sage*, *The Lone Star Ranger*, and *Call of the Canyon*.

George W. P. Hunt (1859–1934) was the first governor of the state of Arizona. He won several terms as governor and was popular with many people for supporting the cause of fair wages for workers.

Helen Hull Jacobs (1908–1997) was a tennis player during the 1920s and 1930s. The native of Globe won the U.S. national singles championship four times in a row. Jacobs was the first woman to wear shorts in professional tennis competition. During World War II, she served in the U.S. Navy as an intelligence officer.

Eusebio Francisco Kino (1645?–1711) explored much of Arizona and served as a Catholic missionary there. He introduced Arizona's Indians to new ways of raising crops and caring for farm animals.

John McCain (born 1936) is a politician who lives in Phoenix. Before going into politics, McCain served in the U.S. Navy and spent five years as a prisoner of war in Vietnam. He has represented Arizona in the U.S. Congress since 1982. The senator ran for U.S. president in 2000 but did not win his party's nomination.

Sandra Day O'Connor

N. Scott Momaday (born 1934) moved with his family to Arizona when he was very young. The part Kiowa and part Cherokee Indian author often writes about the lives of Native Americans. In 1969 he won a Pulitzer Prize for his novel *House Made of Dawn.*

Sandra Day O'Connor (born 1930) has lived in Arizona almost all of her life. After becoming a lawyer, she won election to the Arizona state senate. Later she served as a judge for the Arizona Court of Appeals. In 1981 she was the first woman to be appointed to the Supreme Court of the United States.

Linda Ronstadt

Linda Ronstadt (born 1946) grew up in Tucson and became a famous singer of rock, pop, country, and Mexican music. She has many best-selling albums and has starred in plays on Broadway.

Kerri Strug (born 1977) started competing in gymnastics at age eight. She helped the U.S. women's gymnastics team win their first team gold medal in the 1996 Olympic Games. Strug also won a bronze medal in the 1992 Olympics. She is from Tucson.

Kerri Strug

Clyde William Tombaugh (1906–1997) served as an astronomer at the Lowell Observatory near Flagstaff, Arizona. In 1930 he discovered the planet Pluto by examining a series of photographs taken through the observatory's telescope.

Clyde William Tombaugh

FACTS-AT-A-GLANCE

Nickname: Grand Canyon State

Songs: "Arizona March Song"

Motto: *Ditat Deus* (God Enriches)

Flower: saguaro cactus blossom

Tree: paloverde

Bird: cactus wren

Animal: ringtail

Fish: Apache, or Arizona, trout

Fossil: petrified wood

Gemstone: turquoise

Neckwear: bola tie

Date and ranking of statehood:
    February 14, 1912, the 48th state

Capital: Phoenix

Area: 113,642 square miles

Rank in area, nationwide: 6th

Average January temperature: 41° F

Average July temperature: 80° F

The blue of Arizona's flag is the same blue as the U.S. flag. The 13 rays of red and gold represent the setting sun and the original colonies. The star in the center is copper colored because Arizona is the largest producer of copper in the nation.

POPULATION GROWTH

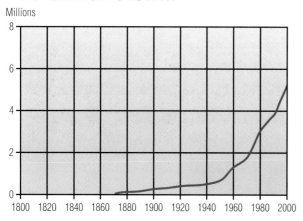

Millions

This chart shows how Arizona's population has grown from 1870 to 2000.

Arizona's motto, "God Enriches," lies in the center of the seal. The scene under the motto represents Arizona's landscape, climate, and industry.

Population: 5,130,632 (2000 census)

Rank in population, nationwide: 20th

Major cities and populations: (2000 census)
Phoenix (1,321,045), Tucson (486,699), Mesa (396,375), Glendale (218,812), Scottsdale (202,705), Chandler (176,581)

U.S. senators: 2

U.S. representatives: 8

Electoral votes: 10

Natural resources: coal, copper, gold, petroleum, pumice, sand and gravel, silver, stone, uranium

Agricultural products: beef cattle, citrus fruits, cotton and cotton seed, dates, hay, lettuce, pecans, wheat

Manufactured goods: electrical equipment, food products, lumber, machinery, metal products, primary metals, printed materials, transportation equipment

WHERE ARIZONANS WORK

Services—67 percent (services include jobs in trade; community, social, and personal services; finance, insurance, and real estate; transportation, communication, and utilities)

Government—13 percent

Manufacturing—9 percent

Construction—7 percent

Agriculture—3 percent

Mining—1 percent

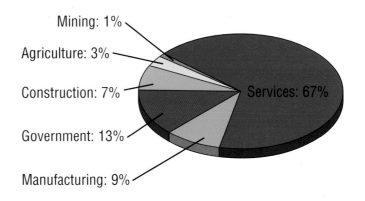

GROSS STATE PRODUCT

Services—64 percent

Manufacturing—14 percent

Government—13 percent

Construction—6 percent

Agriculture—2 percent

Mining—1 percent

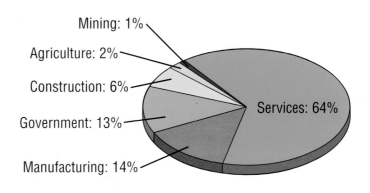

ARIZONA WILDLIFE

Mammals: bighorn sheep, black bear, chisel-toothed kangaroo rat, desert shrew, elk, fox, javelina, mountain sheep, mule deer, porcupine, pronghorn, weasel, white-tailed deer, wildcat

Birds: burrowing owl, cactus wren, dove, great egret, grouse, white-faced ibis, turkey

Amphibians and reptiles: coral snake, desert tortoise, Gila monster, horned lizard, Sonoran desert toad, western diamondback rattlesnake

Fish: bass, bluegill, Colorado River squawfish, crappie, desert Gila sucker, green sunfish, yellow bullhead

Trees: aspen, blue spruce, Chinese parasol tree, cottonwood, Douglas fir, golden raintree, paperbark maple, piñon, ponderosa pine, red maple, rohan European beech, walnut

Wild plants: aloe, barrel cactus, brittlebush, cholla cactus, hedgehog cactus, geranium, golden columbine, organ-pipe cactus, paintbrush, phlox, poppy, prickly pear cactus, saguaro, sand verbena

Roadrunner

Mule deer

PLACES TO VISIT

Apache Trail

This scenic mountain highway is located in the Tonto National Forest, near Phoenix. Indian ruins still stand along the trail.

Arizona-Sonora Desert Museum, west of Tucson

This museum features desert plants and animals native to the region. The museum includes a zoo, a natural history museum, and a botanical garden.

Grand Canyon National Park

One of the natural wonders of the world, the Grand Canyon is 277 miles long, 18 miles wide, and more than 1 mile deep. Visitors can explore the majestic park on foot, by mule, or by rafting on the Colorado River.

Hopi Indian villages, Navajo County

This area includes the oldest continuously inhabited place in the United States. The 800-year-old settlement of Oraibi still stands here.

Kitt Peak National Observatory, southwest of Tucson

This observatory, located on the Papago Indian reservation, has telescopes located on the peak. It houses the world's largest collection of optical telescopes. Visitors can tour the facilities during the day and stargaze at night.

Meteor Crater, Coconino County

Created when a large meteor fell from space, this crater measures 4,180 feet wide by 570 feet deep. A visitor's center offers information about the geology of the crater and the area around it. Hikers can explore the rim of the crater and take in the unusual view.

Painted Desert, northeast Arizona

This stretch of land along the Little Colorado River is named for its colorful rock and sand formations. It is located in the Petrified Forest National Park.

Tombstone

Wyatt Earp was the sheriff in this infamous old western town. Points of interest include the O.K. Corral and a cemetery containing the graves of many famous outlaws.

Residents and visitors can enjoy the ethnic cuisine of Arizona. This woman makes salsa for a contest celebrating the Fiesta de Septiembre.

ANNUAL EVENTS

Cochise Cowboy Poetry & Music Gathering, Sierra Vista—*February*

La Fiesta de los Vaqueros, Tucson—*February*

Great Arizona Outback Chili Cook-Off, Salome—*February*

Cinco de Mayo, statewide—*May*

Wyatt Earp Days, Tombstone—*May*

Frontier Days, Prescott—*July*

White Mountain Apache Fair & Rodeo, Whiteriver—*August*

Navajo Nation Fair, Window Rock—*September*

Fantasy of Lights, Tempe—*November*

Colorado River Crossing Balloon Festival, Yuma—*November*

LEARN MORE ABOUT ARIZONA

BOOKS

General

Blashfield, Jean F. *Arizona.* Danbury, CT: Children's Press, 2000.

Thompson, Kathleen. *Arizona.* Orlando, FL: Raintree/Steck-Vaughn, 1996.

Thybony, Scott. *Arizona.* Portland, OR: Graphic Arts Center Publishing Company, 1990. For older readers.

Special Interest

Cone, Patrick. *Grand Canyon.* Minneapolis, MN: Carolrhoda Books, Inc., 1994. This photo book examines the geologic history of the canyon, including fossils and erosion.

Hoyt-Goldsmith, Diane. *Apache Rodeo.* New York: Holiday House, 1995. Ten-year-old Felicita La Rose lives on the Fort Apache reservation in Arizona. This photo book follows Felicita and her family as they compete in the annual summer rodeo.

Magley, Beverly. *Arizona Wildflowers.* Helena, MT: Falcon Publishing Company, 1992. Learn about some of the more than 3,500 wildflowers that grow in Arizona.

Ross, Michael Elsohn. *Exploring the Earth with John Wesley Powell.* Minneapolis, MN: Carolrhoda Books, Inc., 2000. This biography not only discusses Powell's explorations of the Grand Canyon and the Colorado River but also gives tips on recording data and studying fossils.

Roessel, Marty. *Songs from the Loom: A Navajo Girl Learns to Weave.* Minneapolis, MN: Lerner Publications Company, 1995. In this photo book, ten-year-old Jaclyn learns traditional Navajo rug-weaving from her grandmother, who also teaches her songs and stories about the Navajo.

Fiction

Adler, C.S. *More Than a Horse.* New York: Clarion Books, 1997. Leeann and her mother move to a ranch in Arizona, where Leeann looks forward to riding the horses. After the head wrangler forbids her to ride, Leeann begins working with a therapeutic riding program and adjusts to life in her new home.

Cowley, Joy. *Big Moon Tortilla.* Honesdale, PA: Boyds Mills Press, 1998. Set in a village on the Papago reservation in Arizona, this book follows a child as she learns how to solve her problems by listening to her grandmother, who sings her an old healing song.

Swarthout, Glendon Fred, and Kathryn Swarthout. *Whichaway.* Flagstaff, AZ: Rising Moon, 1997. Set in Arizona in 1920, this novel follows a young boy who is stranded on top of a windmill with two broken legs after a dust storm. Left to die, he ponders his mortality and searches for a way to save his life.

WEBSITES

Arizona @ Your Service
<http://www.state.az.us/>
The official state of Arizona website provides information on services, communities, tourism, and the environment.

Arizona Guide
<http://www.arizonaguide.com>
The official site of the Arizona office of tourism has a trip planner, information on activities and destinations, and maps.

The Arizona Republic
<http://www.arizonarepublic.com>
The website of Phoenix's daily newspaper includes articles of local interest.

Arizona Great Outdoor Recreation Pages
<http://www.gorp.com/gorp/location/az/az.htm>
Articles and information on a variety of parks, trails, and tourist sites in Arizona are provided on this website.

PRONUNCIATION GUIDE

Anasazi (ahn-uh-SAHZ-ee)

Apache (uh-PACH-ee)

Canyon de Chelly (KAN-yuhn duh SHAY)

Gila (HEE-luh)

Hohokam (HO-HO-kahm)

Hopi (HOH-pee)

Mogollon (muhg-ee-OHN)

Navajo (NAV-uh-hoh)

Phoenix (FEE-nihks)

Pima (PEE-muh)

Tucson (TOO-sahn)

The Fiesta Bowl Parade in Phoenix

GLOSSARY

adobe: brick made of clay dried in the sun. The clay is found in Mexico and dry parts of the southwestern United States.

archaeologist: a person who studies ancient times and peoples by digging up what is left of their cities, buildings, tombs, and other remains

canyon: a narrow valley that has steep, rocky cliffs on its sides

colony: a territory ruled by a country some distance away

desert: an area of land that receives only about 10 inches or less of rain or snow a year

groundwater: water that lies beneath the earth's surface. The water comes from rain and snow that seeps through soil into the cracks and other openings in rocks. Groundwater supplies wells and springs.

irrigation: watering land by directing water through canals, ditches, pipes, or sprinklers

missionary: a person sent out by a religious group to spread its beliefs to other people

plateau: a large, relatively flat area that stands above the surrounding land

reservation: public land set aside by the government to be used by Native Americans

treaty: an agreement between two or more groups, usually having to do with peace or trade

INDEX

PHOTO ACKNOWLEDGMENTS

Cover photographs by © Craig Aurness/CORBIS (left, spine, back), © David Muench/CORBIS (right). PresentationMaps, pp. 1, 8, 9, 50; © Wolfgang Kaehler/CORBIS, p. 2-3; © Joe McDonald/CORBIS, p. 3; © Tom Bean, pp. 4 (detail), 6, 7 (detail, left), 19 (detail), 29, 41 (detail, left), 52, 53 (detail); Minneapolis Public Library and Information Center, pp. 7, 21, 49; Thomas Henion, pp. 10, 16, 18, 22, 51, 54; Harriet Vander Meer, pp. 11, 13, 73 (bottom); Sheraton El Conquistador Resort, pp. 12, 43, 47 (both); Ken Palmrose, USDA Forest Service, pp. 14, 57; L. K. Colin, pp. 15, 48 (both), 73 (top); Jerg Kroner, p. 17 (left); S. A. Johnson, pp. 17 (right), 26, 27, 42; Sallie G. Sprague, pp. 23, 32, 58; Smithsonian Institution, pp. 25, 33; Rhode Island School of Design, Museum of Art, p. 28; Arizona Office of Tourism, p. 34; © Tom Bean/CORBIS, p. 35; Arizona Historical Society Museum, pp. 37, 68 (all); © Richard A. Cooke/CORBIS, p. 38; © David Katzenstein/CORBIS, p. 39; © Richard Cummins/CORBIS, p. 40; Phoenix and Valley of the Sun Convention and Visitors Bureau, p. 41 (right); The Museum of Fine Arts, Houston, Gift of Miss Ima Hogg, p. 45; © AFP/CORBIS, p. 46; Nebraska Groundwater Foundation, p. 55; Bureau of Reclamation, p. 56; © Dick Dietrich/Dietrich Stock Photos, Inc., pp. 59, 80; James Payne, Tonto National Forest, p. 61; Tim Seeley, pp. 63, 71, 72; Charles Scribner's Sons, p. 66 (top); Rona Kasen, p. 66 (second from top); Arizona Historical Foundation, p. 66 (second from bottom); Victor Aleman, p. 66 (bottom); © Bettmann/CORBIS, pp. 67 (top, second from bottom); ©CORBIS, p. 67 (second from top); Barry Goldwater, p. 67 (bottom); © Reuters NewMedia Inc./CORBIS, p. 69 (top); James Shea, p. 69 (second from top); AP/Wide World Photos, p. 69 (second from bottom); Lowell Observatory, p. 69 (bottom); © Jeanne Clark/Dietrich Stock Photos Inc., p. 75.